The
Redneck
Wedding Planner

by Mrs. Ophelia Bernice "Sister" Peterson

★ (with a little help from her husband, Buck) ★

Illustrated by Mark Brewer

BROADWAY BOOKS
NEW YORK

This book is dedicated to all us rednecks who know, with absolute certainty, that we rule the day (and night).

BROADWAY

Broadway Books titles may be purchased for business or promotional use or for special sales. For information, please write to: Special Markets Department, Random House, Inc., 1745 Broadway, New York, NY 10019.

Printed in China

BROADWAY BOOKS and its logo, a letter B bisected on the diagonal, are trademarks of Broadway Books, a division of Random House, Inc.

Visit our Web site at www.broadwaybooks.com

The Redneck Wedding Planner is produced by
becker&mayer!, Bellevue, Washington.
www.beckermayer.com

Designed by Katie LeClerq Hackworth

First edition published 2006

Library of Congress Cataloging-in-Publication Data

Peterson, Ophelia Bernice.
The redneck wedding planner / by Ophelia Bernice "Sister" Peterson (with a little help from her husband Buck) ; illustrated by Mark Brewer.— 1st ed.
p. cm.
1. Weddings—Humor. I. Peterson, B. R. II. Brewer, Mark, 1971– III. Title.

PN6231.W37P48 2006
818'.602—dc22

2005042173

ISBN 0-7679-2135-6 (alk. paper)

1 3 5 7 9 10 8 6 4 2

INTRODUCTION

"Ladies and gentlemen, I'm proud to introduce to you for the first time, Mr. and Mrs. Haley "H.C." Blevins IV."

The magic of this moment, when you and your groom are finally declared a couple, joined in love and commitment, celebrated by your friends and family, is one you'll cherish for a long time—at least until the next time you get married.

However, the road to this moment is not one without curves, potholes, drive-by shootings, and cheap motels. Every passage in life requires a guidepost, a trusted friend, a sober family member—and this guidebook is your AA roadmap to your blessed destination.

Wedding planners and consultants from around the country contributed their unique expertise, taking into consideration that what works in Broken Springs, Texas, may not work so well in Squirrel's Nest, Arkansas. Research and persistence pay off no matter where you live.

The details of planning a wedding and a reception are predictable. What's not so predictable is the human element—how you will interact with your family, his family, and your friends. A few words of advice: Be yourself, trust your own judgment, a penny saved is a penny wasted, and if you don't get it right the first time, odds are you'll have many more chances.

Congratulations!

Love,
Sister (and Buck) Peterson

CONTENTS

Chapter Five: PLANNING THE RECEPTION

Chapter Six: THE HONEYMOON AND BEYOND

APPENDIXES

Chapter 1

THE ENGAGEMENT

The Proposal

If you catch wind that your boyfriend might be proposing marriage to you sometime in the near future, try your dangedest to schedule a series of romantic rendezvous in order to push him in the right direction and get him in the mood for wedded bliss.

Top Five Most Romantic Proposal Scenarios:

5 - Announced with a Blue Light Special at K-Mart. Sample:

Attention K-Mart shoppers: Right now in aisle 6, we're featuring a special on Salem Light 100s. And over in aisle 5, Miss Millie Charlene, Harold Lee has a special question for you.

Harold Lee would then get on the loudspeaker and announce his intentions before God and Arnelle Dixon in cosmetics.

4 - Lying in the flatbed of his pickup (or your El Camino), just gazing up at the sky, looking for UFOs.

3 - Painted on the side of his demolition derby car.

Make sure to take a good long look before the derby really gets under way. You might not be able to read anything on the unrecognizable hunk of metal afterward—and, depending on how he fared in the contest, your intended may be something of an unrecognizable hunk himself.

2 - During a whirlwind tour of Branson, Missouri—preferably in the comfort of your recreational vehicle back at Camden Creek RV Park after a spectacular performance of the award-winning Ozark Mountain Jubilee.

1 - After a romantic dinner at the Dairy Queen, when he brings you a derby with the ring hidden under the chocolate shell.

GUY TALK WITH BUCK: ASKING THE PARENTS' PERMISSION

It's customary in some circles to ask the bride's parents for approval. If you have the brains God gave a duck's ass, you'll ask the father first—and do it when he's not watching *Wrasslemania XXX* or *Bubba's "Honey Hole" Bass Fishing Show* on the small screen. You can be sure the mother already knows what's going on.

Tip: There is no need to ask permission if the daughter is disowned, removed from the family home, and/or pruned from the family tree.

The Engagement Ring

Your new engagement ring is the first indication of your husband-to-be's love and commitment, so make sure you follow these tips to get the highest value possible in case the engagement goes sideways.

Diamonds are a gal's best friend:

When your man asks for your birthstone (he won't remember your birthday—get used to it), tell him it's diamond.

Finishing Touch: Make sure he knows that the brighter the stone, the brighter the mood of the bride.

So diamonds weren't in his budget:

The degree of commitment symbolized by diamond substitutes, such as Cubic Zirconium or even a nice, sparkly plastic, can be determined by where they were made:

★ **Made in Guam:** Guam is technically part of the U.S., but it's still only a territory. He's interested for now, but who knows when the excitement of your vast tube-top collection will wear off?

★ **Made in China:** Not only is China very far away, it's also one of the world's oldest civilizations! This is commitment—at least until your sister's divorce goes through.

★ **Made in the U.S.A.:** Jackpot! Your "stone" is superbly cut and polished by the true, the proud, the red, white, and blue—the best gol-danged country in the world. He's in it to win it!

Important Considerations When Choosing an Engagement Ring

The most valuable rings form a complete circle (no matter what the jewelers at the county fair Guess Your Weight Booth say about the "one size fits all" variety!).

1 - When purchasing a diamond, a woman looks at color, clarity, carat, and cut. A man looks at cost to the fourth power, but never mind what he thinks.

2 - Pick the stone that makes the goon break out in a cold sweat.

3 - Pick other areas of the body (including dental locations) that can support diamond chips.

4 - The setting that highlights the stone is one that "sets" it high on the band (see illustration, page 8).

CAUTION: **This ornate setting can easily put an eye out.**

Tip: **Cubic Zirconium is still a popular diamond substitute until the groom gets a real job. Zirconium comes from the word *zargoon*, which means "goat dung fossil" in Arabic and "son of a sick camel" in Persian.**

GUY TALK WITH BUCK:
Ring Options for the Extremely Financially Challenged

An oversized mood ring can also make an attractive and educational symbol of your engagement. Following this scale, you can learn about the many moods of your bride-to-be:

Dark Blue: *Looking for some action.*

Blue: *Thinking about some action.*

Green: *Thinking.*

Amber: *Barely thinking, still stewing.*

Gray: *Not thinking, really stewing.*

Black: *Don't even think about it, you dumb sum' bitch.*

Hint for the Girls from the Mrs.: **A black "mood" will last if the ring stays in the freezer until he gets home!**

The Rules of Engagement

Rule 1: If you're a first-time widow, you should wait a year after your husband's death before promising yourself to another.

Rule 2: If widowhood is your practice or custom, the appropriate waiting periods are determined by a sliding scale of respect for your husband's memory:

- **Second loss**—Wait six months.
- **Third loss**—Wait three months.
- **Fourth loss**—Wait one month.
- **Fifth loss**—Who's counting anymore?

Exception: **This scale only applies when the widow is not held suspect in the loss of multiple husbands.**

Rule 3: If you're a soon-to-be divorcée, you cannot announce your engagement before you and your ex-husband are legally divorced.

Exception: **If the current husband was found in the arms of your very best friend, Judith Ann the tramp, it is perfectly acceptable to physically announce your new engagement to her out back of the dollar store.**

Rule 4: A divorcée also cannot legally marry until her divorce is final.

> **Tip for the Boys from Buck:** While this is federal law, a few rural enclaves in Utah would probably be willing to look the other way.

Rule 5: Be sure to remove the tattoo of your first husband's name before announcing your engagement.

Hint: If removal is too costly and you can't alter the tattoo to make it look like Hubby No. 2's name, a simple "X" through Hubby No. 1's name, followed by a new tattoo of your current man's name, makes a tasteful statement of your devotion.

The Announcement

Place a formal engagement announcement in the local paper, followed by a contact name and phone number.

An example:

Colonel and Mrs. Clyde "Captain" Abernathy of Summom, Louisiana, announce the engagement of their daughter Clydelle to Ellis U. Gooch of Lower Peachtree, Louisiana, and the William Jefferson Clinton Correctional Facility. Miss Abernathy, a graduate of the Toot and Moo Food Service Institute, is an unwanted-hair remover and nail stylist at Betty Jean's Beauty of a Salon. Mr. Gooch is completing the first term toward his Applied Anger Management Certificate. He is the voice of Big Dick's BBQ Burger Drive-In. If all goes well, the wedding will take place in August.

GUY TALK WITH BUCK:

Five Easy Steps to an Inexpensive, Personalized Announcement

Step 1: Choose a short but evocative expression that best conveys your bliss, such as "Lurlene—angels are hard to find" or "Doralee and Junior 4Ever!"

Step 2: Purchase spray paint in day-glo or metallic versions of your wedding colors.

Finishing Touch: If you don't yet know what your wedding colors will be, your local high school colors are an attractive way to proclaim both your love for each other and your support for the home team. Feel free to embellish your announcement with a "Rumpf Rebels Rule!" or an artistic rendering of the school mascot.

Step 3: Select a highly visible town landmark. Train trestles, highway overpasses, and water towers are always popular choices.

Step 4: Drink a sixer of Bud.

Step 5: When good and drunk, paint your joyful news on your landmark of choice in the biggest letters you can manage without losing your balance.

CAUTION: Make sure to choose the least busy time of day to make your announcement. You want it to be a surprise—especially to Sheriff Buford T. Justice.

Dos and Don'ts of
Public Displays of Affection
During the Engagement

★ DO engage in sweet, simple displays of your love, such as strolling hand-in-hand at the mini-mart.

★ DON'T start a game of tonsil hockey under the bleachers during halftime at the high school football game.

Exception: **If other couples are similarly engaged, it would actually be impolite for you not to do the same.**

★ DO check to make sure the preacherman isn't looking before giving your fiancé a love bite at church.

★ DON'T have sexual relations with others even if your other half is in the slammer, fishing, or deer hunting.

★ DON'T under any circumstances allow your public displays of affection to interrupt any NASCAR events, whether you're at the track or in front of the rabbit ears out at Aunt Sissy's duck shack.

Breaking the Engagement

In this unfortunate turn of affairs, the ring must be returned to the groom. Gifts from friends and relatives should be returned with a short note of explanation, such as the following:

Dear Mary Anne,

I regret to tell you that Billy Joe and I have broken our engagement. He is a lying, cheating bastard. Therefore, I am returning the floursack dishcloths you were so sweet to send me.

Love, B.J.

P.S. I will be hanging on to our manufactured home for now.

If the groom-to-be dies before the wedding, the survivor may keep her ring and the gifts given by family or friends unless or until the court-ordered autopsy and court order dictate otherwise.

Chapter 2
PREPARING FOR MARRIED LIFE

Bridal Dowry

In some areas, a wedding without a dowry is considered bad luck. Regardless of wealth, your family can put together a suitable dowry with the following items:

- [ ] A few foreign (Canadian) coins.

- [ ] Lottery ticket (preferably not expired).

- [ ] Some pull-tabs and casino tokens.

- [ ] Hunting privileges with choice of deer stand OR fishing-hole access and an old Evinrude (preferably one that works).

- [ ] Livestock, using the following scale:
  - Good-lookin' gal with a sunny disposition—a chicken and a pack of Juicy Fruit.
  - Mean old gal with a dirty mouth—four cows, two pigs, and a goat.

Tip: **If the bride-to-be is missing any limbs, it's considered polite to throw in a 12-volt battery charger or a cord of wood.**

Dealing with Your New Mother-in-law

The best-case scenario for a young bride is a mother-in-law who is a deaf-mute, living alone and destitute in some middle-of-nowhere place, like California. In lieu of that remote possibility, you must be prepared for her version of "Mother knows best." Your lines of defense:

YOUR GROOM-TO-BE. His behavior at this time could decide everything from the security of your relationship to your future living situation. For example, if your sugar is not only still tied to the apron strings, but also physically hiding behind his momma's apron during these early days of conflict, do NOT plan on parking your doublewide in her yard.

CAUTION: You should NEVER share a septic tank with his momma.

YOUR MOTHER. These early days are the test of how strong-willed and physically strong your momma is. (See the section on gelatin wrestling in Chapter 5.) She will have to play both offense and defense.

YOUR DADDY. He will be noticeably absent in these early days of conflict.

YOU. These early days of dealing with his momma will set the stage for your future married life. In all your dealings with the crusty old (or surprisingly young) bag, be cheerful yet resolute with her childish behavior, be honest yet considerate of her mental illness, and, most important, **do NOT let her handle the wedding presents.**

It's better to beg for forgiveness than ask for permission.

The Combo Engagement Party/ Baby Shower/Bridal Shower

Time and expense are conserved when you combine three ceremonial gatherings. The order of each can be rearranged to fit individual circumstances.

The Engagement Party: Provides the first unsupervised occasion for two families or clans to meet (without weapons) in an informal setting.

Hint: **Coordinating your engagement festivities with one of the regular beer busts out at Cousin Vern's pasture guarantees good attendance.**

The Baby Shower: Celebrates the early arrival of little "Bubbas." Often called a "stork" shower. Suggest general gifts for pre- or immediately after–wedding babies.

Hint: Set up a registry at K-Mart's Another Bun in the Oven section to ensure high-quality gifts.

The Bridal Shower: Focuses the attention back on the bride with a shower of gifts. A gift suggestion could be as simple as a lovely velvet rendering of Hank Williams, Jr. Another creative yet practical idea is to go with theme gifts, such as:

Sex toys: Help build the bride's collection!

Gourmet foods: All-beef bologna, white cheddar or three-cheese macaroni and cheese, and dark bread.

Entertainment for married life: A gift certificate to the Chit Happens Bowling Lanes or the latest in bug-zapping technology.

"GUYS ONLY" SECTION FROM BUCK:
The Bachelor Party

A bachelor or groom's party typically includes only the male members of the wedding party and is typically held where the male members' members can be stimulated without interruption.

> **Safest Place to Seriously Play:** Out on the deer lease or in the duck shack.
>
> **Second Safest Place:** Any girlie bar at least a county away.
>
> **Third Safest Place:** Any casino suite in Nevada.

Tip: **Include husbands and/or boyfriends of the bridal party if you need to spread out the cost of the strippers.**

There are many traditions, handed down from one questionable generation to the next, that are followed at a bachelor party. These vary from region to region, but the most common ones you and your bodyguard (your best man) should be aware of are:

* Holding the groom-to-be down while spot-welding a ball and chain to his ankle.

* Holding the groom-to-be down and shaving all, and I mean all, his body hair.

* Holding the groom-to-be down while going through his pockets for his wallet to pay for the kegs.

Tip: **Any "special" photos of the maid of honor found in your wallet are considered fair game.**

* Holding the groom-to-be down while scanning a copy of *Trailer Park Debutantes* for a clip of the "star" who looks suspiciously like his bride-to-be.

The Bachelorette Party

The pre-wedding gathering of the bridal party, female family, and female close friends serves a dual purpose: getting tipsy and getting naked. Follow this schedule for the optimum bachelorette-party experience:

8 PM Guests arrive.

8:15–8:30 Serve light hors d'oeuvres to keep Grandma busy until the stripper arrives. These can be as simple as Cheese Whiz and Saltines as long as the keg's been tapped, but cocktail weenies are always a classy touch.

8:30 The stripper arrives.

8:31 The stripper is defrocked. (Grandma's in the front—she always wanted to see what the bag boy from the A&P looked like nekkid.)

8:32–11:30 Girls party until they have exhausted all entertainment possibilities—and the stripper.

11:30–? Girls still able to do keg stands go out to get tipsier.

The party officially ends when the bride loses her cocktail weenies—or when Grandma passes out (she's always the last to go).

The Prenuptial Agreement

More and more couples have some legal understanding about what belongs to whom should the marriage take a turn for the worse on the rural route of life. Money-grubbing lawyers like to execute the prenuptial agreements, but these are basically just a list of what you own and what you don't want your man to get his paws on should your happy union go south. You can do it yourself, following these steps:

* **Step 1:** List out everything you own before the wedding.
* **Step 2:** Be sure to specify who is responsible for rented or leased items, such as farm equipment or the velour living-room furniture (you'd hate to see that go back to the store unnecessarily).
* **Step 3:** The key to any prenup is the definition of infidelity. Make sure yours is clear and all-encompassing. "Physical contact" is much too loose a definition. Be specific, and be sure to include phrases like "fooling around," "the horizontal mambo," and "the men's room wall at R.J.'s Truck Stop and Bait Shop."

Chapter 3

DETAILS

Wedding Attire

Wedding Dress

Up until about a hundred years ago, a bride wore the best outfit she already owned. Now brides buy, rent, or borrow their special dresses. Here are some pros and cons to think about when deciding where your dress will come from.

PURCHASE

Pros: Reduces your cost over a long run of marriages.

Cons: Costs a bundle initially.

RENT

Pros: Less expensive initially.

Cons: Think of the questionable women who wore it before you!

BORROW

Pros: Your momma was pregnant when she got married, too!

Cons: See "Rent" above.

Wherever the source, be sure to select the dress that most flatters your shape:

- If you have a small bust, choose a dress with a built-in lift or padded bra.
- If you have a large bust, you are udderly blessed!
- If you have a large behind, select a dress with a long, wide train.
- If you have a small behind, you may be at the wrong wedding.

The details make the dress! Some things to consider when getting gussied up:

UNDERGARMENTS

★ Black thong panties under a white dress are considered a bit tacky.

★ Leopard-skin panties, however, are not.

★ Black bras under a white dress are also on the tacky side.

★ But a glimpse of hot pink or bright blue under the dress can add a colorful touch of class.

Finishing Touch: If your dress is remotely see-through, consider color-coordinating your bra with your bridesmaids' dresses.

★ You'll want to look like an "honest to goodness" woman for your man, so by all means, wear a push-up bra if it will help you bust out of the pack.

JEWELRY

★ Silver snake arm bands are especially appropriate if snakes will be used in the ceremony.

★ Handcuffs should be covered by the bridal bouquet.

★ Necklaces and choke chains should be large enough to go around the neck brace.

VEILS

Veils are symbols of virginity and, thus, are becoming quite rare. The most formal veil size is the four-yard-long "cathedral" length.

Finishing Touch: Attach your veil to a white, lace-embroidered ball cap for an elegantly sporty look.

★ Long trains will require extra attendants as you cross ditches, dirt roads, etc.

★ Long trains also present an exceptional advertising opportunity for a corporate sponsor such as Red Holler's Gun Fun.

★ No shoes, no service.

★ Ankle-strapped spiked heels—*ooh-la-la!*

★ Spurs go with more than cowboy boots.

★ Cowboy boots should be shined and/or oiled.

Something Old, Something New

Even the most modern brides incorporate the Victorian good-luck saying into their wedding wardrobe. Some contemporary suggestions from wedding planner Thomasue "Princess" Puckett of Dry Hole, Oklahoma:

Something Old: A snootful of 100-proof Old Grand Dad.

Something New: The new navel ring you got as a shower gift.

Something Borrowed: A bouquet of the neighbor's hydrangeas.

Something Blue: Powder-blue eyeshadow up to your eyebrows.

A Silver Sixpence in Her Shoe: Have you ever tried to cash a sixpence at the bank? A silver dollar from one of the casinos works better.

Bride's Party Attire

The bride chooses what her attendants wear.

Most Important Consideration: Attendant attire must not steal attention from the bride.

Finishing Touch: If an attendant does go sideways with a dress too short or too low-cut, instruct the head usher to block the tramp's entrance.

Groom's and Groom's Party Formal Wear

UNIFORM

If the groom is employed in uniformed service, dress uniforms are encouraged and will dignify a wedding ceremony. If your honey works for UPS, FedEx, the Postal Service, Shell Oil, or Texaco in particular, encourage him to wear his uniform. These companies provide the perfect wedding attire:

★ Solid-looking uniforms with solid colors (and some with epaulets).

★ Groom's name already embroidered on—no need for a tacky name badge to help you remember which wedding this is.

★ Come with two pair of pants (some with summer shorts) for a wedding in any season.

★ Cleaned free by the company.

★ Present a perfect sponsorship opportunity.

> **Important Tip for the Boys from Buck:** AWOL military should come in civvies.

Buck's Thoughts on Tuxes

The standard approach to a more formal wedding is for the groom and groomsmen to rent or buy their own monkey suits. The disadvantage is that you'll invest in clothing that makes you look like a sissie waiter and won't fit other occasions. Try these tips for choosing multi-occasion attire that looks great:

★ *Have tuxes made from bolts of camouflage-patterned cloth so they can have field use in the spring and fall.*

★ *If your ceremony will be outdoors in cooler weather, line your custom tux with flannel or fleece.*

★ *If your ceremony will be outdoors in warmer weather, line your tux in the new miracle fabrics that conceal human odor.*

Personal Grooming

Hair

The last thing a bride should be doing on her wedding day is worrying about her hairdo. Save time by making Big Hair several days before the event.

BIG HAIR HOW-TO

REGULAR

Step 1: Wash and partially dry hair.

Step 2: Wrap around orange juice or beer cans to eliminate curls and kinks.

Step 3: Cover with a kerchief or tissue paper overnight.

Step 4: In the morning, unravel and back-comb or rat into clumps to be brushed up and smoothed in the shape of a barrel.

Step 5: Spray with lacquer until the dog sneezes.

Step 1: Wash and dry hair thoroughly.

*Hint: **Some girls rinse their hair in sugar water for stiffer hair.***

Step 2: Comb out from the middle, and place an empty 42-oz. can of oatmeal on your head.

Step 3: Comb hair up over the top, and secure in opening with plastic cover.

Step 4: Spray with lacquer until you can't breathe no more.

Tip: **It's common knowledge that the bigger the hair, the longer the marriage.**

Nails

Don't let chewed, broken nails ruin your special day. Try these styling tips for surefire purty nails:

- Grow or artificially extend your nails at least one, if not two inches.
- Paint with the bridal colors and/or metal flake.
- Try embellishing tips with your initials (or his!).
- For ultimate elegance, dangle charms off a few nail tips.
- Spritz with a little fragrance.
- If you're wearing flip-flops, repeat on your toenails.

Makeup

Follow these steps to putting your face on for a picture-perfect day!

Step 1: Start with a good moisturizer.

Step 2: Follow with a good thick foundation.

*Hint: **Choose a base with an orangeish tint for a sun-kissed look.***

Step 3: Add a layer of good thick concealer.

Step 4: Paint on a good thick blush or rouge.

Step 5: Seal with a good clear coat (sold in any local hardware store).

Step 6: Paint lips in something bright and sassy!

Step 7: Line eyes (if eyeliner is not already tattooed on).

Step 8: Apply a good thick coat of mascara—the chunky kind.

Finishing Touch: Highlight your natural features with face glitter.

Invitations

Choosing Your Invitations

Your wedding invitation is your guests' first glimpse at the style of your ceremony. The following rules should help you determine what kind of invitation you should send.

Rule 1: If possible, choose a finely engraved invitation. This will let your girlfriends know you've got a pretty good deal going—whether you really do or not.

Rule 2: Invitations are normally issued by the bride's parents.

Rule 3: If the bride's mother is divorced, widowed, or simply can't find her husband anywhere (even if he was there yesterday!), she is still the one to send the invitation.

Rule 4: If the bride is an orphan or an illegitimate child (father unknown), the invitation should acknowledge everything that is known about where she came from and who raised her. Sample:

THE GREAT STATE OF ALABAMA

REQUESTS THE HONOR OF YOUR PRESENCE

AT THE MARRIAGE OF SOMEONE'S DAUGHTER

Sue Ellen "Elizabeth Ann" Huckleberry

TO

Dwayne "Jim Joe Bob Rebob" McCall

SATURDAY, THE 12TH OF NEVER, AT NOON

HOLY CHRIST ALMIGHTY BAPTIST CHURCH

RURAL ROUTE 1

DELIVERANCE, ALABAMA

Rule 5: Invitations for weddings that are all in the family are, of course, the responsibility of both the bride's and the groom's family. Sample:

MR. AND MRS. CLETUS "ONE EYE" LAMONT, XXIII,

REQUEST THE HONOR OF YOUR PRESENCE

AT THE MARRIAGE OF THEIR DAUGHTER

Shyanne "T.J. R.J. B.J." Lamont

TO THEIR SON

Jethro "Jethro" Lamont

HALLOWEEN NIGHT

BY THE LIGHT OF THE SILVERY MOON

BUB'S MARINA

BIG MOUTH, TENNESSEE

Advice from the Pros: **Leeza Mae, a wedding consultant from Broken Springs Honeymoon Planning, suggests saving money by making a poster-sized budget invitation with tear-off telephone numbers and posting it on the Wal-Mart community bulletin board.**

The Invite List

The final invite list is a compilation of four earlier lists—one each from the bride, groom, bride's family, and groom's family. Some considerations when planning the size of your wedding and whom to invite:

★ If both you and the groom are from the local area, your invite list will have some overlap.

★ If you two are distant cousins, your list could shrink enough to allow you to invite former boyfriends.

★ Ex-wives and ex-husbands should not be invited.

Exception: **If your ex is also a family member and your wedding, for all practical purposes, is just another family reunion, said party must be invited.**

DON'T be afraid to set limits as to how many rugrats can attend.

DO add a note, such as, "Please bring no more than fifteen children," to your invitation.

Wedding Rings

The first question to ask is where to buy your ring—a neighborhood jeweler, Wal-Mart, or a trusted street dealer? After that, it's all about style.

- Rings of value are made of metal. Therefore, a steel washer can make for a high-quality wedding band.
- A solid gold ring can become a family heirloom, especially when the gold comes from sentimental sources.

  Tip: **It takes about twenty gold fillings to hand-fashion a decent band—think about that before you close the casket on old Uncle Cletus.**

- A gold-plated band will turn your finger green, whereas a silver band complements braces and nearby body piercings.

Tip: **These alternatives are also great in case one of you lost your left hand in a tragic altercation with a combine and can't really support a wedding ring.**

- A set of nickel-plated broken-heart necklaces engraved with the words "True Love"—you get one half, he gets the other.

- His and her tattoos—you get his name, he gets yours.

  Finishing Touch: Get a tattoo artist to do a "live" inking during the course of the ceremony to really let your loved ones share this intimate moment with you—and to keep them entertained during the boring parts of the ceremony.

- A pair of dog tags emblazoned with a moving slogan like "God Bless the U.S.A."

- Matching tongue studs.

  CAUTION: **Do NOT get these done during the ceremony—it's very difficult to say your vows with a piercing artist's hand in your mouth.**

Photography

Just in case Uncle Bubba's been right all along and the federalis do monitor photo labs for evidence of illegal activity, Polaroid ceremony and (especially) reception photos are probably better for all concerned. Otherwise, keep costs in focus when deciding if you want to hire a professional to capture the high points of the day.

Finishing Touch: If at all possible, hire a photographer from one of those Civil War photo booths at the county fair and get him to bring along his props to add a touching bit of pride and history to your wedding memories.

> **Hint for the Boys from Buck:** Try draping a Confederate flag in the background and having the boys wear fake beards and/or long wigs to give the groom's party photo a whisper of Lynyrd Skynyrd.

Flowers

Fresh flowers are the best, yet most expensive, expression of love, hope, and happiness. Costs can be managed by making sure you choose flowers that are in season and local.

SOME SHOPPING SUGGESTIONS

★ **A neighbor's flower garden:** You can be sure that when they return from vacation, they will be pleased that their prize-winning roses played such an important role in your wedding.

★ **Funeral homes and catering services:** Almost-fresh flowers can be purchased after important events at a major discount. Get in good and early with the custodian.

★ **Cemeteries:** For the best arrangements at the best price, stop by after a remembrance day. Flags are a special bonus.

Tip: ***Cemetery custodians go home at dusk.***

The high cost of fresh floral decorations can also be nipped in the bud by using dried or silk flowers, either of which can be sprayed with a lovely aerosol scent.

Hint: **If cost is a major concern, freshly blown-up party balloons in soft pastel colors can be twisted to look like flower bouquets.**

Ceremony Decorations

In formal settings, ceremony floral arrangements are always white. More casual weddings have a wider palette to choose from. Try these tips to personalize and beautify your venue:

★ Coordinate the ceremony flowers with the personal camouflage of the groom's tux. Pink tulips and red roses, for example, bring out the autumn hues in late-season camo.

★ Alternate red gardenias, white Calla lilies, and blue spray-painted daisies throughout the venue for a patriotic feel.

★ Have pussy willows dyed to match your momma and your new mother-in-law's dress colors (magenta and fire-engine red, respectively), then intertwine throughout the church as a symbol of your respect—and a reminder that they mind their manners toward each other during the reception.

Wedding Party Flowers

Bridesmaids' bouquets are similar in style and color to the bride's, but smaller and of lower quality. For example, if the bride carries a fresh bouquet of exploding milkweed, the bridesmaids will carry plastic imitations.

The groom's party and father all wear a boutonniere in their lapel. Any flower except cauliflower is appropriate for the men.

- Dandelions wrapped loosely in silvery leaves of sage.
- Smaller grain crops from the family farm, such as a sprig of flax or a slender stalk of wheat.
- A bud of cannabis is a smashing complement to any suit.

Finishing Touch: Hide several toothpicks in the arrangement for easy access.

Reception Decorations

Four-legged animals can be made into interesting mounts in lieu of floral centerpieces. Centerpieces should "fit" the table linen. For example, if the table linen is woodland camo, don't use stuffed ducks as a centerpiece (unless they are wood ducks). Use stuffed chipmunks or squirrels.

Hint: **Lacy shower curtains make fine tablecloths and provide an elegant backdrop for inspired taxidermy artistry.**

Finishing Touch: Ask the taxidermist to mount one large gray squirrel and one smaller red squirrel, holding hands, to represent the wedding couple.

Transportation

Arrange transportation to and from the ceremony and/or reception site in advance and with an eye to style. If, for example, you are both horse lovers, arrive on separate horses and depart on the groom's horse.

Tip for the Boys from Buck: Untrained horses will bolt if you blast a road sign on the way to the ceremony.

Some General Transportation Guidelines

1 - The bride and groom should arrive at different times—but on the same day.

2 - The family arranges the bride's arrival, with her father riding "shotgun."

3 - The bride and groom's vehicle must be the highest off the ground.

The wedding party's vehicles must be at least six inches lower than the couple's.

Guest vehicles must be an additional six inches lower than the wedding party's.

4 - No unusual, upstaging jerry-rigs (one end elevated, bouncing shocks, etc.) in the newlyweds' Monster Truck Marriage Parade.

5 - Only the bride, groom, and ceremonial animals are allowed in the departure vehicle.

> **Finishing Touch from Buck:** If you rent or "borrow" a school bus to transport the wedding party, make sure the windows open at least halfway in case there should be any road signs or critters along the route that need plugging.

Music

Ceremony Music

★ **Prelude:** If you're getting married at the VFW, a kickin' house band is probably included in the hall rental fee, and they can entertain the crowd while you finish spot-welding your big hair.

CAUTION: DO NOT, under any circumstances, allow the band to play "Dueling Banjos" or "The Devil Went Down to Georgia" this early in the ceremony—you'll have a riot on your hands for sure. Firmly instruct them to stick to the Carter Family and maybe a little Allman Brothers.

★ **Processional:** Try to get your hands on a bootleg of Travis Tritt's cover of the "Wedding March."

CAUTION: Do not let the organist (AKA Judith Ann the tramp's second cousin) slip in "The Other Woman" at the bride's entrance.

★ Recessional: A personal favorite of many groomsmen is "Free Bird." But any number by Willy, Waylon, and the boys is appropriate.

*Advice from the Pros: **Polly Dardon, an impressionist/wedding planner from Branson, Missouri, recommends karaoke singing by the audience for a personalized recessional. Their choices should be pre-screened.***

Reception Music

Reception music is less traditional. As important as the music is how you want it played. The following definitions will help you determine who should perform your reception music:

Soloist: One person singing karaoke.

Duet: The result of a rare birth condition (unless the doctors have already cut them apart).

Quartet: The result of fertility drugs.

Chamber Ensemble: Group of windy string musicians who specialize in music to sleep by.

Guidelines for Including Animals in Your Ceremony

Large Mammals

* Horses

Tip: **Couples arriving and/or having their ceremony on horseback should provide a small clean-up detail.**

Hint: *Lesser in-laws are a perfect choice for this assignment.*

* Hogs and cattle (see "Civil Ceremonies, Unusual Circumstances" in the next chapter)
* Asses (see groom's family)

Small Mammals

Domestic pets can be nicely incorporated in a ceremony as:

* Ring dogs
* Dogs of honor
* Guard dogs for the gift table and portable bars
* Choral accompaniment ("Ol' Blue and the Coonhounds")

Chapter 4

PLANNING THE CEREMONY

The Dos and Don'ts of Choosing A Date for Your Ceremony

You'll get more husbands and boyfriends to come during hunting/fishing off-season, so confirm the dates with your local game warden. Otherwise, keep the following considerations in mind when picking the perfect date for your special day:

- **DO** be sure to avoid any and all NASCAR event dates.
- **DON'T** select any potential Super Bowl dates.
- **DON'T** select any potential New Orleans, GMAC, Tangerine, Fort Worth, Alamo, Houston, Music City, Sun, Motor City, Liberty, Continental Tire, Sugar, Holiday, Independence, Outback, Gator, FedEx, Capitol One, Rose, Orange, Cotton, Peach, or Fiesta Bowl dates either.
- **DO** be sure to check tour schedules for Willy, Garth, Shania, Dolly, and any other country icon (including the Oak Ridge Boys).
- And most important, **DO** be sure to plan around Aunt Flo's monthly visit.

When choosing a day of the week, Saturday is preferred because most of your guests can attend a weekend event. Sunday mornings are busy enough for most pastors, but Sunday afternoons are a viable option, especially if the county has loose liquor laws.

Selecting the Type of Ceremony

There are two basic choices—a religious or a civil ceremony—but the two are not necessarily exclusive of each other.

1 - Religious Ceremonies

Religious ceremonies can be very civil, provided you take the following precautions:

★ Make sure you have enough ushers to quell disturbances from outside agitators. (See the section on ushers under "Selecting the Wedding Party.")

★ Set up a weapons check at the door.

★ Keep your exes from sitting near the aisle. Make sure they're boxed in good and tight between members of the local chapter of the Ladies Auxiliary.

Tip: **A church setting will most likely have a temporary overall calming effect on the family clans.**

2 - Civil Ceremonies

A civil ceremony is often the choice of a couple in unusual circumstances, such as:

★ One or more of the parties is a Yankee.

★ One or more of the parties has been in a bad farm/mine/oil-rig accident.

★ One or more of the parties is a seventh-year freshman in high school.

★ One of the parties is a large animal.

Choosing a Venue

If you can't get married where you first met (over a steaming plate of grits at the Waffle House) or where you've spent much of your time since (the buffet line at Shoney's), you have plenty of other options.

Churches

If guests are disarmed at the door and a few of his family members are sedated, a church wedding can be a lovely, serene affair even in your own United "Save Me Almighty Jesus Before Satan Takes My Soul, Hallelujah!" Baptist Church. If you aren't a member of any church, most pastors will rent their churches out if they sense a reward down here on Earth. (Even if you are a member, the pastor won't recognize the groom, although he's referred to him often enough as the "bad seed" in the reading of the Gospels.)

GUY TALK WITH BUCK:
Dos and Don'ts for Shotgun-Wedding Firearm Safety

For practical reasons, not to mention concealment purposes, many fathers are leaning toward the use of handguns in these barely civil ceremonies. Remember, the guiding principles of firearm safety are:

★ DON'T point a firearm at someone unless you mean to.

★ DO roll the window down all the way before shooting.

★ DON'T shoot the warden's dog.

Clubs

Your daddy's service or social club might be the right choice for you, especially if he can split the pull-tab revenue with the bar.

The Elks, Moose, Eagles, and Masonic lodges all come formally decorated.

Hint: If the regulars refuse to give up their bar stools, put screens around or a blanket over them.

Other Public Buildings

There are alternative, less costly wedding venues. The best of these is usually the local high school due to its wide range of options; for example, you could get married in the gym and have the reception in the cafeteria.

Tip: **As a taxpayer, you have every right to ask the cafeteria manager for some of that federal food surplus.**

And just like when you were in school, the library stacks make for a quiet, deserted oasis in case other couples are inspired enough by your first dance as a couple to do a horizontal hula of their own.

Finishing Touch: Reassure guests who "graduated early" that truancy laws are not in place during a civil ceremony.

Tip: **If you plan to use a public space, like a fancy hotel lobby or the greeting area of the new Wal-Mart for your wedding, it's best to let the owner/manager know beforehand.**

Hint: If you are planning an outdoor event, check the forecast in the **Farmers Almanac.** *If, however, on the day of the wedding, the pigs are tossing their bedding and the dairy cow is lying in the yard, move the event indoors.*

Your Venue Preparation Problems Solved

Problem 1: My aisle runner looks pretty, but falls apart whenever anyone steps on it.

Solution: *Use cloth as the aisle runner. Colorful as they are, Christmas wrap and newspaper just don't hold up.*

Problem 2: I can't get the tape that's holding my aisle runner down to stick.

Solution: *Make sure the floors are swept clean of sawdust, cigarette butts, and peanut shells before applying tape.*

Problem 3: I want to have my ceremony outdoors, but at my last outdoor wedding, nobody knew where they were supposed to walk or sit.

Solution: *First, mow closer to the ground (or, for starters, mow at all). Then use ball-diamond chalk to mark the outline of an aisle.*

Problem 4: I want to have my wedding in the backyard, but the backyard's a cornfield.

Solution: *Make sure not only to pick, but also to chop cornstalks for a simple, charming ceremony atmosphere.*

Home Weddings

CAUTION: **This section is recommended for doublewide owners only—unless your wedding will be a small affair held in the middle of the night and attended only by the preacher, your cousin/husband-to-be, your daddy, and his 12-gauge.**

Advantage: You save money.

Disadvantage: You'll be at home (and if you've followed this book to the letter, everyone in town will know it) and, therefore, available to receive eviction notices, subpoenas, handcuffs, etc.

Prison Weddings

If your fiancé is unjustly/justly behind bars, your wedding will also take place behind a set of bars. Each prison has different rules, but the following checklist should help you plan your special maximum-security day:

☐ Obtain the prison's marriage packet, which should include policies and procedures, a fee schedule, a list of approved chaplains, and one ribbed condom.

☐ Pick a date on which you already have a conjugal visit scheduled (otherwise your man gets to celebrate your wedding night with a giant poster of Daisy Duke).

☐ Check cake, gifts, and any other wedding materials for metal objects (they will be scanned, and a pocket-knife pie could delay your special day).

☐ Bring a friend who is on your fiancé's approved list or find an inmate or guard who's able to sign his name to act as a witness.

Selecting the Wedding Party

Maid of Honor

Most brides prefer to pick their best friend as maid of honor, but many yield to the old saying "blood is thicker than water" and pick a family member, such as a sister.

CAUTION: **Avoid generations of bad blood over troubled water.**

Bridesmaids

The bridesmaid selection process is typically guided by three criteria:

1 - Number: The bride can have as many attendants as she'd like, but a good rule of thumb is one bridesmaid for every usher—unless an usher requests two for good measure.

2 - Family or friends?: Family obligations can be fulfilled via the maid of honor—just keep in mind the frequency of family reunions (and, therefore, frequent attempts on your life for not appointing enough cousins as bridesmaids). However, friends are equally eager to join in on an almost-free party— and if they aren't selected, to let their fists tell you how they feel about it at the local watering hole.

3 - Physical appearance: Make sure that none are prettier, taller, smarter, or bustier than you. Those who are can stay at home that day or be put in charge of the dowry livestock.

CAUTION: **Some female family members and girlfriends will be disappointed at not being chosen no matter how you disguise the real reason (wrong eye color, too many freckles, etc.).**

*Hint: **Appease disgruntled cousins by asking them to serve as "supervisor" of the stripper at the bachelorette party.***

Buck's Guidelines for Selecting the Best Man

★ The best man should be your best buddy, family or not.

★ The best man should be trustworthy in the deer woods, on rough waters, and when the bar fights begin.

★ The best man acts as your "dittohead"—covering your tracks whenever, wherever.

Ushers

RULE OF THUMB: Plan one usher for every 50 expected guests and one armed usher for every 150 guests.

For extra security, select only your largest friends and family members as ushers, and at least one should be an experienced dog handler. In special circumstances, ask the Sheriff to deputize several ushers and have these individuals wear the badge under their boutonnieres.

Other Roles

There will be those who feel left out by not being selected to join the wedding party. Depending on how close they really are, these individuals can be asked to:

★ Emcee the reception tractor pull.

★ Sing a special song during the karaoke recessional.

★ Be a bar-back at the reception.

★ Pick the neighbor's flowers when they aren't looking.

★ Tend the coon dogs under the front porch.

Un-selecting a Bridal Party Member

If you find out that your maid of honor, Judith Ann the tramp, has been having relations with your husband-to-be, she should be disinvited either verbally or in writing.

Hint: **Make sure the ushers get a picture of each disinvited individual prior to the ceremony so diversionary tactics can be deployed.**

Ceremony Elements and Schedule

Pre-Ceremony Checklist

ONE HOUR BEFORE THE CEREMONY

- [ ] Ushers make last-minute adjustments to boutonnieres and check to be sure their flies are zipped.
- [ ] Bridesmaids adjust their undergarments.

THIRTY MINUTES BEFORE THE CEREMONY

- [ ] Prelude music begins.
- [ ] Seating begins.
  - Guests check handguns, throwing knives, Arkansas toothpicks, and other self-defense/-offense items.
  - Ex-spouses are quickly ushered to the county jail for violating the restraining order.
  - Guests for the bride are seated on the left.
  - Guests for the groom are seated on the right.
  - Guests with probation officers are seated in the rear.
  - Higher-risk guests are tethered to large tree out back.

- [ ] Groom and best man arrive.
- [ ] Family and other drinkers arrive and are seated.
- [ ] Groom's mother makes a final, furtive plea to her son not to go through with it.
- [ ] Bride does a last-minute check to make sure her mascara hasn't run, her lipstick isn't on her teeth, and her fishnets have no obvious holes.

The Processional

1 - At the top of the chosen hour, the music starts and the preacher moves to face the audience.

2 - The groom and his best man follow to face the music.

3 - Bridesmaids begin the long walk.

> ❀ The marching order of bridesmaids is simple: smallest to tallest, least pregnant to most pregnant.

The grand moment of the wedding ceremony is when the bride begins her walk, on the arm of her father, toward the altar.

> **Hint for the Boys from Buck:** It's helpful to have two people assisting the bride along if she is showing some resistance to the ceremony.

Double-Wedding Processional Procedure

- If the mother of the bride has finally decided to double the family's joy and marry the man she sleeps with most often, she will go first on the arm of her son.
- If the two brides are sisters and both are pregnant, both will be on the arm of the father of the baby.
- If the two sisters are joined at the hip, a private civil ceremony is recommended.

Housekeeping Notes

In addition to being the wedding officiate, preachers are ultimately responsible for their facilities, so a few short housekeeping announcements before the ceremony are becoming much more common. Some suggestions:

NO FIGHTING

HUNTING DOGS SHOULD BE LEFT UNDER THE FRONT PORCH

NO CARVING INITIALS IN THE PEWS

TURN OFF ALL WEATHER RADIOS AND POLICE SCANNERS

Betrothal

The ceremony starts with the traditional:

We are gathered here in the sight of God and these witnesses to unite Billy Joe and Bobby Jo in holy matrimony. As proud, God-fearing Americans and (thank you, Jesus) true believers, they recognize that a church wedding by an underpaid minister of the cloth is serious stuff indeed. The love expressed in the vows is the love that you can only find on Days of Our Lives. *They know that the role of spouse is like a dinner roll—well-prepared, then baked*

just right. They also know that a good marriage runs like a
rebuilt Trans-Am: The road may be rough, but the custom shocks
will protect you.

The preacher concludes with the traditional, *"Who giveth this woman to be married?"* The father and/or mother then steps forward.

Hint: **Some uppity women do not like to be "giveth away" by anyone. "Whose child is this?" is a great alternative—unless the question will be met with an uncomfortable silence from the congregation.**

Vows

Vows should not be more than three minutes long each or the crowd will turn on you—count on it. Vows are significant to you, but they're also important to the audience, who often only hear certain words. They will be listening for phrases like "remote control," "candlelit TV trays," "joint gun racks," and "old dogs and children and watermelon wine."

Traditional vow sample:

I (groom) take you (bride) to be my lawfully wedded old lady, and I do promise and covenant to be your loving and faithless husband, to provide you with as much deer meat and catfish as you can eat, to listen to you carefully so I can understand what the heck you're thinking, to let your momma visit when I'm out fishing; for better, for a lot worse; for richer, for a lot poorer; in sickness and in awful health so long as we both shall live in the same doublewide, huh?

Ring Exchange

Objections

At this point, it's traditional for the preacher to say, "If anyone gathered here today knows any reason why these two should not be joined in holy matrimony, speak now or forever hold your peace." A significant amount of time can be saved by replacing "speak now or forever hold your peace" with "then what the hell you doin' here?" If you've decided on the more formal wedding, any unpleasantness can be avoided by having the head usher cue the airhorn section of the choir just as Judith Ann the tramp opens her big mouth.

Prayer

The preacher asks the audience to quiet the rugrats for a prayer. Sample:

Eternal Father, God, Creator of the Lunker and big bucks, we ask your blessing on this newly formed union. May you protect them and their kin from aliens and other out-of-towners. May you also watch over their manufactured home, outbuildings, ATVs, and livestock. May they always turn to you first, the lottery second, and family last in times of great financial need. May the revenuers never find your secret stash. We ask this in his name, your humble, under-paid disciple (me).

The Kiss

Most newlyweds don't
need prompting for a
kiss, but in the ceremony
at least, it should usually
be preceded by the preacher's
statement, "You may now kiss the bride."

Hint: **Make sure you turn your new hubby so his back is to Judith Ann**
the tramp, who may try to take this opportunity to mouth plans to him
for a secret reception rendezvous.

Introduction

After a kiss that's long enough to make Judith Ann good and
jealous, but just shy of embarrassing your momma in front of
her quilting bee, the preacher will say something like:

"It is my great privilege to introduce to you for the first time, Mr. and Mrs.
Ray Boyce Culhane, Sr."

Recessional

At the conclusion of the ceremony, the organist will start
playing the recessional and the wedding party will leave the
ceremony area in reverse order of their arrival.

Important Tip: **Guests (especially those who had a sixer before the**
ceremony) are extremely restless by this time, and the speediest
exit of the wedding party is encouraged.

Even More Important Tip: **Any seated guest planning to participate**
in the ceremonial dove shoot must be allowed to exit the chamber first.

Receiving Line

The receiving line includes only the bride, the groom, and their parents—and the largest usher at the front of the line to guarantee the safety of the newlyweds.

Tip: **If while in the line, an obviously smitten boy-man whispers, "Gal, we'd go together like stank on a skunk," graciously decline and quickly turn to the next guest.**

Grand-Exit Dove Shoot

The release of white doves as symbols of love and peace when the new bride and groom exit the church can be a magnificent testimony to their vows and a loving display of skill by friends whose previously checked guns are now waiting conveniently at the front door. The code of conduct for these dove shoots is:

- ★ No shooting caged birds.
- ★ There must be blue sky under your first target.
- ★ No rifles if you are near a federally supervised airport.
- ★ No paintball guns—it confuses the birds.
- ★ No Civil War cannons—unless everyone uses one.
- ★ Bird dogs may retrieve, but not bury or eat downed doves.
- ★ Don't let ex-spouses handle the guns.

Finishing Touch: An evening shoot is exceptional entertainment, especially if there are iron shavings in the reloads.

*Tip: **As soon as they fall, the doves from this shoot should be breasted and wrapped in bacon for the reception grill by the ushers. (See "Food" in the following chapter.)***

Preparing for the Inevitable

Emotional Outbursts

The music and emotion stirred by the ceremony may move audience members in different ways. You can count on hearing a selection of the following outbursts and/or "whispered" comments:

- ❧ 'Bout time!
- ❧ Well, butter my butt, and call me a biscuit!
- ❧ Yer darn tootin'!
- ❧ He fell out of the ugly tree and hit every branch on the way down, bless his heart!
- ❧ Sur 'nuf!
- ❧ A gal like that is scarcer than hen's teeth!

Additionally, the more sensitive may have an alternative religious experience during the ceremony.

Problem: If it's a bright, sunshiny day, Elvis and/or the Holy Mother may pass through the stained, cracked, or broken church glass to reveal themselves in mysterious ways.
Solution: Let those with sightings enjoy their exclusive view in silence. Those celebrating not in silence during the ceremony should be hushed up one way or another.

Problem: Speaking in tongues is a touchy subject since true believers hold "tongues" as divine communication.
Solution: A good pastor should remark in his housekeeping comments that mumbling in tongues is acceptable during the service, but shouting is not.

Problem: Any guest may start barking like a dog at any time.
Solution: Have an usher take that person, with or without leash, outside to play with the other dogs.

Fighting

Sometime during your special day, a fight(s) will break out. It may be as simple as a family member defending your honor or opening a can of whoop-ass for no reason at all. Try these tips for managing tempers on your special day:

1 - Ask the preacher to make an announcement that if guests must fight, it has to be outside.

2 - Keep a bucket of water handy.

3 - Keep a case of pepper spray handy for larger disturbances.

4 - Keep a cattle prod handy for the groom's family.

5 - Keep the wedding party's blood types handy.

The most vicious wedding fighting will be between your mother and his, fueled by his mother's opinion of your mother and her trashy daughter (you). Wedding planners advise keeping these two women separate unless mud wrestling is planned as entertainment.

Finishing Touch: A scheduled fight at the reception will guarantee a memorable wedding day. See "Buck's Alternative Entertainment Options" in the Reception chapter.

Dress Code

Most of your guests will dress according to the occasion. But you know darn well there will be some who will dress according to their circumstances (often dire), some who will dress for effect, and, most disruptive, some who will undress for effect. Be clear: **NO SHIRT, NO SHOES, NO BOOZE.**

Postponements

If for some reason you wish or need to postpone your special day, it's most polite to let your guests know well in advance with a simple card or announcement in the local paper. Sample:

The marriage between Don Roy Puckett and Isolene Cummins will not take place by order of the U.S. Department of Human Genetics. Department officials would only comment that their gene pool needs a new filter.

Chapter 5
PLANNING THE RECEPTION

Seating Arrangements

The guest seating for the reception is divided between Them (your guests) and Us (the wedding party). The following considerations ensure a relatively violence-free reception:

* The wedding party sits at a lengthy head table, often elevated, in the most visible location.
* Relatives and other special guests are seated at reserved round tables clustered near the head table, with distance determined by guests' closeness or familiarity with the newlyweds and/or throwing-arm ability.
* Less-special guests have to find their own dang seat.
* High-risk guests are spoon-fed their last meal somewhere outside.

Hint: **If families are going to be mixed at guest tables, make sure weapons are re-checked at the reception door.**

Even Bigger Hint: **Set up a wire mesh protective screen in front of the head table before the toasting begins.**

Favors

Thank special guests with a small token of your affection. A keepsake placed at each table setting will remind everyone of his or her participation in your special day. The best keep-sakes are homemade. Some suggestions:

- A Mason jar of home brew
- Mr. Potato Head made with potatoes from your own garden
- A few 30/30 or 12-gauge handloads
- 3″ x 5″ recipe cards from the event
- A jar of Geraldine's green pepper jelly or, better yet, a quart of her bread-and-butter pickles

*Hint: **Place favors in inverted John Deere ball caps or miniature feed bags.***

Finishing Touch: Place two or three cigarettes wrapped with ribbons in the bridal colors at every other place setting.

Food

The food served following the ceremony is a substantial part of your wedding budget. The four most common food presentations are:

1 - Hors d'oeuvres: a snack for Yankees and other idiots. French for "not enough food."

2 - Buffet dinner: like open-field running through a restaurant, picking up food from the cook line and other guest plates. Your position at the starting gate is all-important.

3 - Seated dinner or "plated service": a plate full of warm stuff already dished up in the back hall and served to you by people who consider your reception hazardous duty.

4 - Tailgate party: stand-up affair outside (where good food belongs), amid the toys that make life worth living.

How To Save Money on Your Reception

* Have your reception from 11:00 AM to 2:00 PM. It's easy to dress up a buffet line of soups and sandwiches, and lunch portions are smaller than those at dinner.

* Have your reception from 6:00 AM to 9:00 AM after a lovely sunrise service. This early event could be inexpensively catered by Waffle House.

Finishing Touch: Tell the boy at the counter to add sprinkles to match the wedding colors.

* Have a reception centered around a theme, such as NASCAR. Place the kegs and cheap racetrack-style junk food (hotdogs made from sawdust and beef juice, corn chips slathered with warm cheese slime) in "pit-stops" near the shade-tree mechanics ripping apart R.J.'s transmissions out back. Have the older "drivers" wear #3, the younger #8.

Hors d'oeuvres

Hors d'oeuvres, also known in some fancy circles as *"canopies,"* are the first course of your reception food, placed on tables around the reception area and accompanied by napkins and toothpicks.

Suggested menu items:

* Cocktail weenies on toothpicks
* Boiled goobers
* Jerky and meat sticks
* Alligator on a stick
* Rocky Mountain oysters
* Pickled pigs' feet
* Ham hocks
* Dove breasts from the church killing grounds wrapped in bacon strips and broiled on the grill

Finishing Touch: Nothing demonstrates your hospitality better than a large Velveeta cheese log.

*Hint: **Three-pound bags of wholesale-club potato chips will keep the expectin' gals busy for hours—and away from the more expensive chow.***

Lunch and Dinner Menus

A sit-down wedding lunch is different from a dinner in that portions are smaller and lunch includes only two or three side dishes, whereas a dinner offers many choices. A side dish may be specially prepared from entrée scraps.

Some suggestions:

- ★ Fried mullet with a side of fried mullet backbones (AKA cracker popsicles)
- ★ Deep-pit/spit-roasted pig with a side of cracklings
- ★ Catfish—fried
- ★ Game meat—slow-roasted

SIDE DISHES

- ★ Cheese grits
- ★ Hush puppies
- ★ Sliced onions
- ★ Okra, collard greens, turnip greens—breaded or fried
- ★ Goobers
- ★ Jello salad in the wedding colors
- ★ Tater tots
- ★ Sausage gravy
- ★ Corn chips

GAME MEAT

Game meat is a surefire money-saver. Tell your husband-to-be how many animals you'll need for the reception at least a month prior to the wedding. If the warden shows up at your reception, make sure the groom and ushers are prepared to answer any seemingly casual questions he may have.

Buck's Guide to Game Meats

Deer: Bambi and his mother are the signature wild-game entrée and the most cost-efficient game animal to work with. Some tips:

- Do not cook venison with the skin on—especially fawns with spots—as this has the tendency to upset Yankee guests and other dipsticks.
- Save the backstrap for the wedding party.
- Reserve any "gut-shot" meats for exes.

Raccoon: Ol' Blue and his scattered offspring will bring many "masked bandits" to bay for the reception. Roast raccoon at the end of the buffet line is a dramatic dish, especially when accompanied by a fine piece of taxidermy. A mount of a raccoon washing its little hands in a soup bowl is a sure attention-grabber.

Finishing Touch: A photo of your prized blue-tick treeing a coon nicely completes the picture.

Possum: This mild-mannered animal is so easy to collect, it seems they are born dead alongside the road. Roast possum as you would any small animal. Tastes a lot like porcupine.

CAUTION: Plentiful as they are, it just takes too many possums to make a main course. Reserve these critters for appetizers.

Guidelines for Collecting Reception Roadkill

★ The best shopping hours are at dawn and dusk.

★ Collect only the freshest roadkill—warm to the touch, but not because of the sun.

★ If you've hit a doe, back up and wait for the buck.

★ Barnyards are a good source of chickens, geese, and an occasional turkey.

★ Gut and clean animals at earliest convenience.

★ Breast out birds at earliest convenience, out of sight.

★ Remove feathers and animal body parts from grill and undercarriage.

★ Meat from small domestic pets who have passed on should not be wasted.

(Contributed by Rusty Peterson, Founder and Executive Director, Meals Under Wheels Foundation.)

Special Diets

★ High salt: certainly available throughout the reception hall.

★ Low salt: certainly unavailable, whatever it is.

★ Yankee: crow, any way they want it.

★ Atkins: Trace doesn't have a special diet, as far as we know.

★ Low carb: one barrel or two?

Beverages

Guests return to the buffet table only once or twice, but most will drink at least the cash equivalent of their wedding gift at the bars. You can control some of the consumption with several time-tested techniques:

- Drink tickets for one or two free drinks, then cash bar only
- Cash bar only
- Short-pour
- Short glasses
- No change given

If you have to buy your alcohol from the facility, you have three payment options:

1 - Pay by the individual drink.

CAUTION: **Challenges the bartender's counting skills.**

2 - Pay by the bottle.

CAUTION: **Can lead to dangerous over-pouring.**

Hint: **Make sure bartenders don't give out full bottles.**

3 - Pay per person.

Your Best Option: **This is the most cost-effective choice, especially if the facility proprietors don't know either of your families.**

Kegs

Kegs come in three standard sizes:

1 - The $^1/_2$-barrel "full keg"

2 -The $^1/_4$-barrel "pony keg"

3 - The $^1/_6$-barrel "sissy keg"

Tip: **Imported beer kegs are either 30 or 50 liters, whatever liters are and wherever Canada is.**

Hint: The full "American" keg, which contains $15^1/_2$ gallons of beer, will either serve one 12-oz. glass to 160 guests or the ushers prior to the ceremony.

Kegs require a deposit, so for this and other security issues, chain beverage containers through the taps to the washtubs. Then chain the tubs to a tree, clothesline, or tailgate.

CAUTION: **Unless set in cement, children's swing-sets are simply not secure enough to chain a keg to.**

Some Cost Considerations When Setting Up the Bar

★ Put the beer keg, glasses, and napkins on the front table.

★ Keep all other booze on the back table.

★ Surround the back table and side entrance with garbage cans.

★ Use only plastic glasses. His side will bring their own 72-oz. Big Gulp cups.

★ Provide each bartender with garnishes, a corkscrew, a bottle opener, a sponge, a can of Mace, and a wooden baseball bat.

Beer in Other Forms

* **Longnecks:** Longneck Buds are most appreciated, but a longneck can become a weapon handle for the more violent members of the wedding party.
* **Plastic bottles:** Beer doesn't taste as good in plastic bottles, but they don't break when thrown across the room.
* **Cans:** Cans, when crushed against the forehead, result in far less garbage than bottles.

Champagne

Champagne is the traditional toast beverage—and also easily gargled away with a Bud or Busch longneck.

Hint: **To stretch the champagne, dilute with up to 50% carbonated soda water.**

CAUTION: **All carbonated beverages should be chilled and never publicly shaken.**

Liquor

Mixed drinks and shots are expensive—in both hard cost and property damage—to serve. For public safety reasons, serve only beer and wine. There will be enough "panther's breath" available out in the parking lot to slake any serious thirst.

Hint: **If you must serve hard liquor, make sure it's brown and that it starts with a man's name, like Jim or Jack or "Old."**

Punch

Punch may be an acceptable alternative to mixed drinks or beer and wine in some areas. This is not the case in your hometown. Punch without alcohol is for children, Yankees, and other idiots.

Wine

Wedding planners advise the formula of two-thirds white to one-third red wine when planning reception consumption. If you are featuring red game meat (squirrel, raccoon, deer) on the buffet line, reverse the formula. If you have any rhubarb wine, throw that in, too.

Smart Shopping Tip: **If real wine is being served on the sly in church facilities, buy it (tax-free) through the pastor.**

Be sure to order wine familiar to the groom's family: Mad Dog 20/20, Wild Irish Rose, Night Train Express, and "What's the Word?" Thunderbird. Screw-top wines ensure top quality.

Bar Etiquette

When adult beverages are involved, manners hinge on when the bar opens and closes. You can ensure your guests' good behavior by following two simple rules:

1 - DO NOT OPEN THE BAR UNTIL
THE BRIDE AND GROOM ARRIVE.

2 - ONCE OPEN, DO NOT LEAVE BAR UNATTENDED!

Tip: **For safety reasons, place soft drinks for the kids who are not yet drinking and the adults on liver dialysis a good distance away from the bar.**

Toasts

The best man traditionally gives the first toast, offering some-thing personal about his connection to the groom, such as:

Your new bride had three children by me. I know you're gonna enjoy being married to her! I sure 'nuff did—and so did Bobby Ray, Ray Bob, and Bobby Joe! Here's to your happiness and our exit off the deadbeat-dads rosters!!

The best man is followed by the groom, the bride, and the parents.

Sample Toasts

★ For the groom who is a duck hunter: "If it flies, it dies."

★ For the groom who is a deer hunter: "If it's brown, it's down."

★ For the bride: "The perfect bride is a diplomat in the living room, a skinflint in the kitchen, and a wildcat in the bedroom."

Toasting Ground Rules

Rule 1: Those who toast must stand and, if necessary, hold onto something solid.

Rule 2: Those receiving a toast must remain seated—unless the toast includes a family insult.

Rule 3: If any family members currently in the care of a correctional institution wish to make a toast, a conference call to a speakerphone at the head table should be arranged with the assistance of the warden at least seven days in advance.

Finishing Touch: Include a seven-second delay feature so non-celebratory comments can be edited out.

Rule 4: Short toasts can be shouted out from the floor until you direct the DJ to start the music.

CAUTION: Do not pass the DJ's microphone through the crowd. You know how agitated an audience gets when Springer does that.

Wedding Cakes

The earliest wedding cakes were little wheat cakes broken over the bride's head for good luck. Some modern choices:

- ♦ Multiple-tier cake: modeled after the spire of St. Bride's Church in London, England.
- ♦ Flat cake: modeled after the parking lot of the new Wal-Mart.

Cutting the Cake

The newlyweds make the first cut of their wedding cake. The proceedings of this small ceremony are guided by superstitions:

- ♦ The first cut must be along the cake's centerline or the couple will not equally share the joys and trials of married life.

Finishing Touch: Whether it's a favorite skinning knife with stag handle, Daddy's military Bowie knife, or great-great-granddaddy's Rebel ceremonial sword, use your special family cutlery to slice the wedding cake.

- Each places cake in the mouth of the other. It's not a good sign if one cuts a big piece and smashes it into the face of the other.
- If a single woman places a piece of cake under her pillow, she will dream of her future husband.
- If a single woman wakes up to find her piece of cake smashed beneath her the next morning, it's quite likely her future husband is drooling on the pillow next to her.

GUY TALK WITH BUCK:
Groom's Cakes—Have Your Own Cake and Eat It Too

A groom's cake is usually a chocolate sheet cake with chocolate frosting and, as many are hoping, possibly containing liquor. Groom's cakes come in many shapes too:

- ★ Alma-mater football
- ★ Big-screen TV iced with the logo of your favorite outdoor program
- ★ Armadillo or possum
- ★ Your favorite oversized "Rebel Yell" belt buckle

Tossing the Bouquet and the Garter

The Dos and Don'ts of the Bridal Bouquet Toss

- ◆ **DON'T** throw away an expensive bouquet to some tramp in the crowd.
- ◆ **DO** have an accomplice slip you a substitute bouquet of plastic flowers when you turn your back on the group.
- ◆ **DO** station one of the armed ushers at the edge of the crowd to keep married women, women older than 70, and men out of the catch zone.

GUY TALK WITH BUCK: The Garter Toss

Some big-city wedding consultants consider the garter belt toss outdated and slightly vulgar. Screw them.

Step 1: Remove the garter (pocketing any money tucked in there) and any other undergarments of your choosing.

Step 2: Throw the garter to the boys on the dance floor. Whoever catches it is the next to marry, although not necessarily to the girl who caught the bridal bouquet.

Step 3: The recipient then hangs the garter from the rearview mirror of his F150 to convince the ladies of his prowess.

Dancing

1 - The first dance is reserved for the bride and the groom.

2 - The second dance is usually for the bride and her father.

Tip: **If the bride has both a birth father and multiple stepfathers, a family line dance is a perfectly acceptable substitute.**

3 - The groom and his mother also take a turn around the floor during the father-daughter dance.

Important Hint: **Watch his mother like a hawk during this dance—she may make a last-ditch effort to grab her baby and make a run for the hill country.**

Money Dance

The money or dollar dance is a nice way for the bride and groom to make a little extra coin toward their honeymoon or parts for the outboard motor.

Step 1: The best man and bride dance together.

Step 2: While dancing, the best man pins a dollar to the bride's dress. If he doesn't have a pin, he'll stick the dollar somewhere in the bride's bodice, or the bride will put the bill in her pantyhose.

Step 3: Guests are invited to "pay" for dances in like fashion.

Tip: **If a guest stuffs a fiver down your front, make sure he understands it's for five non-consecutive dances and absolutely NO lap dances.**

★ **DON'T** take checks—out-of-town or local.

★ **DON'T** make change.

★ **DO** discount Canadian and Mexican money—make sure you get your full U.S. dollar's worth.

★ **DON'T** take coins smaller than a quarter.

BUCK'S ALTERNATIVE ENTERTAINMENT OPTIONS

Tractor Pull

This entertainment can run concurrently with the reception and is supervised by the groom's ushers. To be officially sanctioned by the International Association of Pud Pullers, the following categories must be offered:

* Two- and four-wheeled
* Gasoline-, diesel-, and alcohol-fueled
* Stock and super-stock
* Modified and super-modified

In addition, pud-puller sleds must be equipped with sidebars for participants to grab onto.

Scheduled Fights

If you schedule a fight as entertainment during the reception, your wedding day will be long remembered. Once feigned good manners wear thin, Ed "Beercan" Drizzle of Rebel Wedding Planners recommends a "strip fight" in which, after each round of two women fighting, the loser removes a garment. The fight continues until one combatant is nekkid as a jaybird. At that point, the crowd is the winner.

Finishing Touch: Gelatin is always a tasteful wrestling substance. The addition of canned fruit qualifies the mixture as a reception side dish.

Gifts

Some guests will not have sent or delivered their gift to you prior to the wedding, and an area should be set aside for these gifts. Place a large table away from the front door or emergency exits and assign a member of the wedding party to make sure all gifts received have an attached card and that none are left by ex-husbands/wives. Livestock should be caged or tethered outside.

Gift Security

The usher with the tracking dogs stands near the gift-table area during the entire reception, and by the truck while the loot is loaded at the end of the event. There will be guests who want to exchange a gift or say they are part of the bride's family and are just "helping" with gift storage.

our honeymoon!

Chapter 6
THE HONEYMOON AND BEYOND

The Honeymoon

For any number of reasons (a disappointing money dance, parole violation, etc.), your honeymoon may be best spent nearby. Bonus: You may even have enough for two nights at one of these local options:

- Betty's Bid-A-Wee-Wee Bungalows, downstream from the Senator Clucker's Chicken Plucking Plant and down the road from two Denny's and a Stuckey's
- The Shangri-La Motor Lodge and Miniature Golf Resort at Defunk Springs
- Gomer and Verlene's B&B Gator Farm

Save the big trips—a pilgrimage to the Big Bopper's Reconstructed Crash Site or an intimate, passionate tribute to the King in a truck-stop bathroom near Graceland—for your first anniversary.

The honeymoon is a critical period for many newlyweds, as traditions (some good, some not so good) become habits. Honeymoons have two parts: the wedding night and the long day after.

THINGS TO DO ON YOUR WEDDING NIGHT

1 - Crack the windows on the pickup so the dogs can breathe, and put some water in their dish.

2 - Have your man carry you across the threshold to your first wedded night of reckoning.

Tip for the Boys from Buck: You'll have to set your new wife down to give the desk clerk your expired, over-limit credit card.

3 - Hang the "Do Not Disturb and I Really Mean It" sign on the outside knob. Then jam a chair under the inside knob, and don't open the door unless you see flashing red lights.

4 - The operative word for the wedding night is CONSUMMATION. The ceremony isn't legal until consummated.

THINGS TO DO THE MORNING AFTER

1 - Greet your new spouse with, "I did *what?*"

2 - Open your gifts and decide whose gift is worthy of a thank-you card and whose isn't.

3 - Do some more consummating.

THINGS TO DO THE MORNING AFTER THE MORNING AFTER

1 - Sneak out in the early hours, dropping the room key in the slot before the clerk can see you.

2 - Return gifts for cash value wherever possible.

3 - Get the gelatin stains out of your wedding dress as best you can, and return it to the rental store.

4 - Start mentally preparing yourself for life with his momma.

The Annulment

There are any number of reasons to annul a marriage, the least of which is the groom's inability to do some good, old-fashioned consummating on the wedding night. The most common reason for annulment is that the marriage wasn't valid to begin with. These marriages are treated as if they never happened, and the parties involved are still considered single. Invalid marriages include:

★ Unions between parties who are already married to other parties.

★ Unions between parents and children, brothers and sisters, uncles and nephews, and any other shirttail relatives.

★ Unions involving a spouse who is a few beers short of a six-pack and, therefore, can't give proper consent.

Important Tip: **Even if consent was obtained through some sort of hocus-pocus from a fast-talking flim-flam man, this marriage can still be considered invalid.**

* Unions between a human party and a large domestic or circus animal party.
* Unions involving any kind of alleged alien abduction.

CAUTION: Alien abduction has been notoriously difficult to prove in court—even if it's *The People's Court*.

D-I-V-O-R-C-E

D-i-v-o-r-c-e is another matter all together and usually occurs soon after Judith Ann the tramp whispers in your new husband's ear, *"I want to rev your engine, Mr. Newlywed, Mr. Hot Shot, Mr. Demo Derby King. If you let me, I won't tell your wife. If you don't, I'll tell her you did anyway."*

Tip for the Boys from Buck: Another common cause of d-i-v-o-r-c-e is the birth of a red-headed stranger.

Tip for the Girls from the Mrs.: **If mitigating factors (kids, a *Walker, Texas Ranger* video collection, a joint down payment on a choice set of ceramic yard ornaments) are involved, try to work out your differences before you run to Judge Judy.**

In general, keep in mind that marriage is a commitment that takes work, and that d-i-v-o-r-c-e is a last resort that can be pure h-e-double-l for the both of you. Before you take this drastic step, think about all the care you lavish on your El Camino, or how devoted he is to his best coon dog, and see if you can't try treating each other with the same love and respect. After all, you've come this far—and you don't really want to look for Hubby No. 6 at this stage in life, do you?

APPENDIXES

Appendix A: To-Do List

Twelve months before the wedding

- [ ] Stop day-dreaming about Richard Petty, and start looking for a man who's a little more attainable.

Nine months and three days before the wedding

- [ ] Let your boyfriend get to first base.

Nine months and two days before the wedding

- [ ] Let your boyfriend get to second base.

Nine months and one day before the wedding

- [ ] Let your boyfriend get to third base.

Nine months before the wedding

- [ ] Let your boyfriend "come on home."
- [ ] Begin planning your honeymoon.

Eight months before the wedding

- [ ] Let your boyfriend know he hit a home run.
- [ ] Get him to propose.
- [ ] Remove any embarrassing tattoos.

Seven months before the wedding

- [ ] Let your husband-to-be know he's benched for the season.
- [ ] Start planning engagement festivities.

Six months before the wedding

- [ ] Send invitations.
- [ ] "Forget" to invite the Yankee side of the family.

One month before the wedding

- [ ] Start clearing some of the junk out of the yard and frontroom.
- [ ] Send as much as you can bear to part with to the dump with your fiancé—and instruct him to trade it in for "new" junk in the wedding colors.

One week before the wedding

- [ ] Have ceremony dogs checked for rabies.

Six days before the wedding

- [ ] Put in an emergency call to the home-shopping channel for that hair-removal system you've had your eye on.

Five days before the wedding

- [ ] Move the cinder-blocked cars out of front yard—or decorate them in the wedding colors.

Four days before the wedding

- [ ] Check air in truck tires.
- [ ] Hide all wedding vehicles in shed.

Three days before the wedding

- [ ] Dig cock-fighting pit.
- [ ] Start making gelatin for the wrestling pool.

Two days before the wedding

- [ ] Have grandma retouch your eyeliner tattoos and restick your press-on nails.

One day before the wedding

- [ ] Place first-aid kits in strategic locations and behind portable bars.

The morning of the wedding

- [ ] Release groom from leg irons.

Appendix B: Budget Worksheet

There are several budgeting methods you can use to help plan your first wedding. One common method is to divide and list for each item the bride's estimate, the groom's estimate, and the actual cost. **Example:**

ITEM	BRIDE'S ESTIMATE	GROOM'S ESTIMATE	ACTUAL
Wedding Rings	$10,000	$100	$10

Another popular method is to use a pie chart. For example: 75% booze, 7.5% food, 15% bride and her bridal party, 1.5% groom, and 1% reserve for the bailbondsman. Whatever you decide, both families share responsibilities for payment.

Hint: **It may seem rude at the time, but have his side of the family pay by cashier's check.**

Responsibility of the Bride and Her Family

- Bride's dress
- Any missing teeth
- Venue rentals and flowers
- Reception food and refreshments
- Groom's ring
- Bride's fake ID
- Cake
- Toe rings for the bridesmaids

Responsibility of the Groom and His Family

- Bride's engagement ring
- Bride's wedding ring
- Groom's tux
- Tornado-proofing the wedding couple's doublewide
- First lap dance at the bachelor party
- Personal flowers
- Rehearsal dinner
- Groom's fake ID

Other

- The bride's party pays for their own dresses.
- The groom's party pays for the "hostesses" at the bachelor party.

Appendix C:
Tips for Financing Your Wedding

Weddings can be very expensive, but many modern brides find the cash in creative ways. Try these options before you auction off his ATV when he's out of town:

Have a car wash (trucks, tractors, and boats, too)!

* Your bridesmaids all must wear bikinis.
  Hint: Topless car washes bring in the biggest tips.

Hold a bake sale!

* Make a sign with a picture of Uncle Eddy after the horse accident. Write "BENEFIT FUNDRAISER" across the top.
* Go to the day-old store and stock up on any week-old baked item that doesn't sport a brand.
* Unwrap and sell off the curb.

Set up kissing booths!

* At planned events: the county fair, church socials, motorcycle rallies, VFW fish fries, the Fourth of July parade, Civil War reenactments.
* On spontaneous occasions: at bus stops, train terminals, hospital waiting rooms, busy traffic intersections.
* Attendant kissing booths at the rehearsal dinner and reception.
  Tip: You can get in on this action, too. Just be discreet, and try to kiss no more than one of your new husband's brothers.

Have a yard/trailer park sale!

* If you advertise this as an estate sale, you'll end up with fewer coins.

* To sell to those driving a car less than ten years old, place little placards near an item containing "information" about the item, like a short history of how the toilet cozie saved the life of your grandpappy, the late senator.

Sell advertising space on the ceremonial transportation!

* Your locally owned Dairy King, Piggly Jiggly, Acme Rehab Center, and Rice Farmers Co-op are all excellent prospects.

Broadcast your honeymoon as a live Internet feed!

* Or go the old-fashioned route—just set up a camcorder and make copies to sell to the groomsmen.

Acknowledgments

The authors wish to thank and absolve all involved in this caper. Additional free-drink tickets are being held at the door for "Big Mack," "Skeeter," "Beercan," "Scarlett," "Lamb," "Snortin' Horton," "GayLee LayLee," "Sourdough," "Pearl," "Dot," the inmates of the Alabama State Girls Home for the Young and Reckless, "Dorothy the Hunting Pig," Elmo "Excuse Me" Farquar, "Leeza," and, of course, any number of Buck's old girlfriends barely disguised as "Judith Ann."

About the Authors

Buck Peterson, master guide to all-that-is-wild-in-the-outdoors, has traditionally offered marriage counseling to his hunting and fishing buddies on an ad-hoc basis, most often in the Valhalla lounge of his hunting lodge on Big Babe Lake (go to www.buckpeterson.com for reservations). In this exciting new guide to weddings, his latest wife, professional bride Mrs. Ophelia Bernice "Sister" Peterson, has captured Buck's lodge-spun wisdom between covers. More important, she has inserted her six-bits of experience for the modern bride. Sister has a hard-earned black belt in the marital martial arts, and is often referred to as the "Wallah of Wedding Planning" and "that woman" in divorce proceedings. She is the musical director of The Altar Girls, a contract wedding karaoke group, and confidant personal wedding-dress shopper for a few notable women and even more less notable women.